THE BOY WHO WENT TO THE LIBRARY

By ALTON CARTER

Illustrations by JANELDA LANE

The Boy Who Went to the Library
Copyright © 2018 by Alton Carter

Published by Monocle Press, a division of Strata Leadership, LLC
11600 Broadway Ext. Ste. 220, Oklahoma City, OK 73114
www.monoclepress.com

Design by Qubit Creative

JNF002000 JUVENILE NONFICTION ADVENTURE & ADVENTURES
JNF007050 JUVENILE NONFICTION BIOGRAPHY & AUTOBIOGRAPHY

978-1-7321189-7-3

This book is dedicated to all the librarians who are helping students use their

IMAGINATION

to see the world
in a whole new way.

My teacher said,
"Alton, I know what you need...

take a trip to the library
and find something to read!"

I ran down the hallway
and out the front door...

the bus to the library
was bus number four!

I got on the bus with no time to spare.

After six stops, I was finally there!

I saw books everywhere
when I walked in the door...

books in every room
from ceiling to floor!

There were books on tables,
books on shelves...

books about trolls,
and books about elves!

Books about science, weather, and rocks...

I saw books about hats, pants, and socks!

I never imagined
there'd be so many books...

books and more books
everywhere I looked!

Books about people called
biographies...

there were books about toads,
monkeys, and bees!

Books about maps,
books about towns...

books about elephants,
peanuts, and clowns!

Some books had pictures,
some just had words...

some books had paintings
of flowers and birds.

Books about history
and world leaders' faces...

I loved the books
about faraway places!

Books made of paper,
books made of cloth...

books with hard backs
and books that were soft!

Books about the moon
and books about the sun...

my teacher was right,
THE LIBRARY IS FUN!

We invite you to draw yourself
doing something that uses your

IMAGINATION!

When the picture is complete,
send a copy to
www.theboywhodreamedbig.com
so we can share it with the world!

Printed in the USA
CPSIA information can be obtained
at www.ICGtesting.com
LVHW052302160124
768957LV00017B/78